Don't Step on the Sky

A HANDFUL OF HAIKU

Miriam Chaikin   ILLUSTRATED BY **Hiroe Nakata**

HENRY HOLT AND COMPANY • NEW YORK

For my greats—
Elise Sarah Pearl, Adam Dylan Pearl,
and Samuel Chaikin Colman—
with love from Grant Molly   —M. C.

For my grandma
who wrote haiku every day   —H. N.

Henry Holt and Company, LLC
Publishers since 1866
115 West 18th Street, New York, New York 10011

Henry Holt is a registered trademark of Henry Holt and Company, LLC
Text copyright © 2002 by Miriam Chaikin
Illustrations copyright © 2002 by Hiroe Nakata
All rights reserved.
Distributed in Canada by H. B. Fenn and Company Ltd.

Library of Congress Cataloging-in-Publication Data
Chaikin, Miriam. Don't step on the sky: a handful of haiku / by Miriam Chaikin;
illustrations by Hiroe Nakata. 1. Haiku, American. 2. Children's poetry, American.
3. Nature—Juvenile poetry. [1. Haiku. 2. American poetry. 3. Nature—Poetry.]
I. Nakata, Hiroe, ill. II. Title.
PS3553.H24272 D66 2002 811'.54—dc21 2001001469

ISBN 0-8050-6474-5 / First Edition—2002 / Designed by Donna Mark
Printed in the United States of America on acid-free paper. ∞
10 9 8 7 6 5 4 3 2 1

The artist used watercolor and ink on Arches paper
to create the illustrations for this book.

ABOUT THE POEMS IN THIS BOOK

Haiku is an ancient form of Japanese poetry that has become popular throughout the world. The word in Japanese means something like "playful verse." A haiku is usually about nature—trees, streams, birds. It may be serious or funny. A traditional haiku is written in three lines, with a total of seventeen syllables:

> On the first line, five
> On the second line, seven
> On the third, five more.

The last line is often surprising.

In modern times, rules for writing haiku have become more flexible. Today, a haiku may have fewer than seventeen syllables. It may be written in one or two lines, even four.

However many lines or syllables, the aims of haiku remain the same—to capture a moving experience in a few words.

Here is a handful of poems in the haiku tradition.

—M. C.

Early morning,
a lone crow on a high post:
caw caw empty world.

Light gray, dark gray:
day asleep.
Orange, yellow:
day awake.

Duck glides across pond—
water doesn't notice.

No rain. Flowers droop.
drip
  drip
    drip
Ready to play!

An inch
of blue ribbon
flies in—
pipes twice—
flies out again.

My favorite? Hmmm.
My eyes love geranium.
My nose loves freesia.

Lovely lily
alive for only a day.
Take good care of yourself.

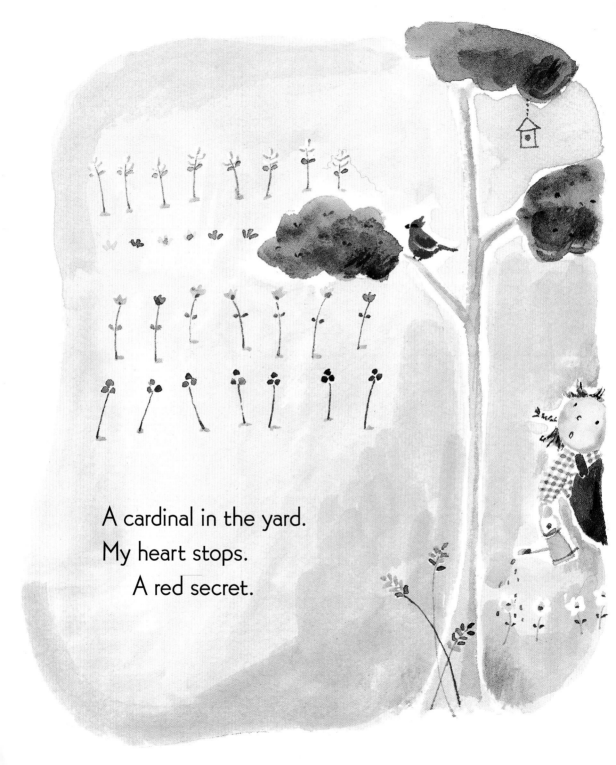

A cardinal in the yard.
My heart stops.
  A red secret.

A blade of grass
pushes through cement.
Hello, world.

Not only caterpillars.
Buds become flowers,
flowers, fruit.

Bamboo tree,
how fast you grow.
    Yesterday
    I was taller than you.

A grain of rice marches uphill—
on the back of an ant.

Slug. Be more like your
cousin snail.
Put some clothes on
when you go walking.

The birds. I hear
their happiness,
but . . .
where are they?

I have a cat,
her name's Nasturtium.
She's my cat,
I'm her person.

A brook rushing
over stones—
the sound of happiness.

Seagull
flies and cries,
flies and cries.
All gulls come to look.

The sea runs to the shore.
On shore, they run to the sea.
Both are happy.

Clouds play tag with skyscraper.
Skyscraper waits its turn.
Waits . . . and waits . . . and waits.

The cat sits on her haunches,
watching the street.
How like an eggplant!

Orange smokestack
moves through the fog.
But where is the river?

Why is the river
running away?
I see no one chasing it.

Rain. At last!
How happy the grass is.
   Me too.

Rain strikes sidewalk.
Sidewalk strikes back.
It is raining up!

Night lights.
Raindrops on my window.
A gallery of diamonds.

The windows keep me
awake all night,
arguing with the wind.

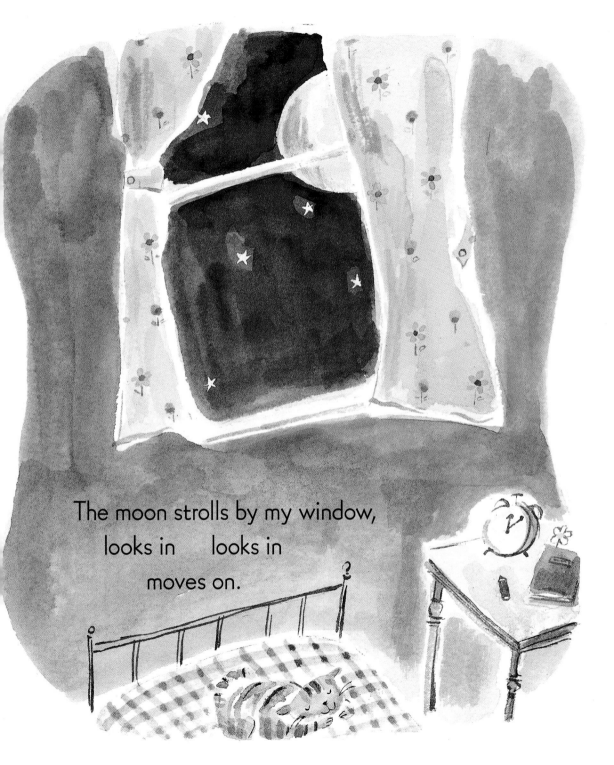

The moon strolls by my window,
looks in   looks in
moves on.

Rain, the path
that was here
yesterday,
where did you put it?

After the rain
a puddle.
　Careful.
Don't step on the sky.